GRAPHIC NONFICTION
CLEOPATRA
THE LIFE OF AN EGYPTIAN QUEEN

by
GARY JEFFREY & ANITA GANERI

illustrated by
ROSS WATTON

BOOK HOUSE

Designed and produced by
David West ☆☆ Children's Books,
7 Princeton Court,
55 Felsham Road,
London, SW15 1AZ

Editor: Gail Bushnell
Photo Research: Carlotta Cooper

Photo credits:
Pages 4, 45 (both) – Mary Evans Picture Library
Pages 6 (bottom), 44 (top) – Rex Features Ltd.

First published in 2005 by **Book House**,
an imprint of **The Salariya Book Company Ltd**
25 Marlborough Place, Brighton BN1 1UB

Please visit the Salariya Book Company at:
www.salariya.com

HB ISBN 1 904642 89 6
PB ISBN 1 904642 90 X

Visit our website at **www.book-house.co.uk**
for free electronic versions of:
You wouldn't want to be an Egyptian Mummy!
You wouldn't want to be a Roman Gladiator!
Avoid joining Shackleton's Polar Expedition!

Due to the changing nature of internet links, the Salariya Book Company has
developed an online list of websites related to the subject of this book. This site is
updated regularly. Please use this link to access the list:
http://www.book-house.co.uk/gnf/cleo

A catalogue record for this book is available from the British Library.

Printed on paper from sustainable forests.

Manufactured in China.

CONTENTS

WHO'S WHO

Cleopatra VII (c. 70-30 BC) Queen of Egypt and the last of the Ptolemaic dynasty. With Mark Antony, she was defeated by Octavian at the Battle of Actium in 31 BC.

Julius Caesar (c. 100-44 BC) Brilliant Roman politician, general, and writer. He conquered Gaul and invaded Britain. He made himself dictator and was assassinated on 15th March, 44 BC.

Protarchus (*dates unknown*) Cleopatra's chief adviser. Very little is known about him, but he held the post of prime minister in 51-50 BC.

Mark Antony (82-30 BC) Roman soldier and politician. He ruled Egypt with Cleopatra after Caesar's death. Following their defeat by the Romans, he committed suicide.

Octavian (ruled 31 BC-AD 14) Adopted son and heir of Julius Caesar. He defeated Cleopatra and Mark Antony at the Battle of Actium. He later became the first Roman emperor, known as Augustus.

Quintus Dellius (*dates unknown*) A Roman historian and friend of Antony's who later sided with Octavian.

THE ANCIENT EAST

Cleopatra tried to rebuild the great empire of her ancestors, the Ptolemies. In 34 BC, at a special ceremony of Donations in Alexandria, she and her children were given back many lost lands. Just four years later, however, Cleopatra's empire fell to Rome.

THE EMPIRE OF THE PTOLEMIES

When Alexander the Great died in 323 BC, the Greek general Ptolemy was made governor of his lands in Egypt. In 305 BC, Ptolemy became pharaoh and founded a new dynasty. The Ptolemies ruled Egypt for almost 300 years. Under Ptolemy II (282-246 BC), the empire was strong. Ptolemy II expanded Egypt's lands and riches. But in the second century BC, royal power was weakened by invasions, taxes, and dishonest government. Meanwhile, the threat of Roman power was growing stronger.

FAMOUS ANCESTORS
One of Cleopatra's most famous ancestors was Queen Arsinoe II. She was sister and wife of Ptolemy II who reigned from 280-246 BC.

ALEXANDRIA
CAPITAL OF THE ANCIENT WORLD
The city of Alexandria was the Ptolemies' capital in Egypt. It was founded by Alexander the Great in 331 BC. With its fine harbour, it became a great centre of trade and business. A lighthouse stood on the harbour island of Pharos, which was linked to the mainland by a causeway. The city was famous for culture and learning. It had an enormous library that was used by scholars from all over the ancient world.

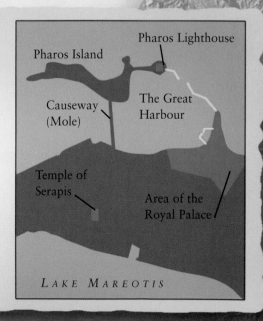

Pharos Island

Pharos Lighthouse

Causeway (Mole)

The Great Harbour

Temple of Serapis

Area of the Royal Palace

LAKE MAREOTIS

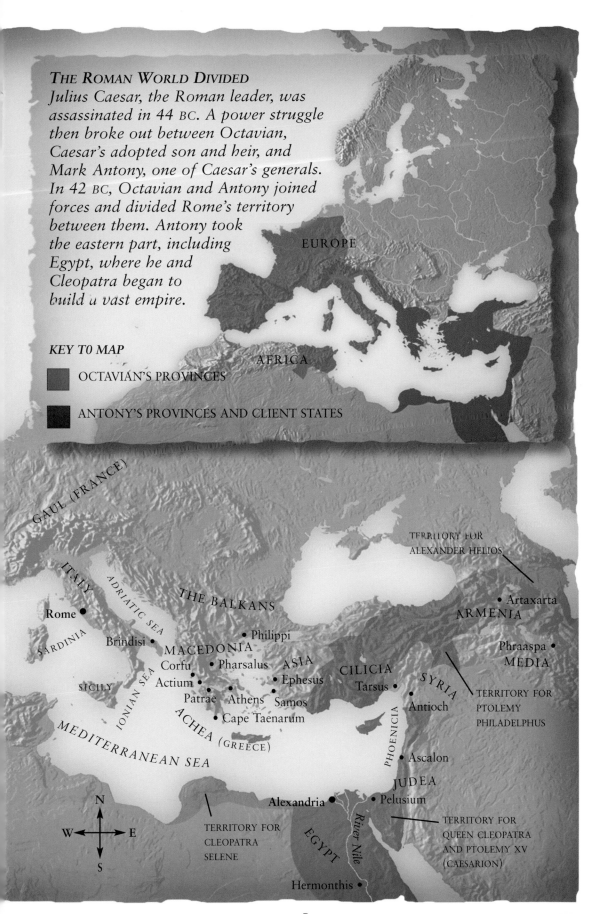

THE ROMAN WORLD DIVIDED

Julius Caesar, the Roman leader, was assassinated in 44 BC. A power struggle then broke out between Octavian, Caesar's adopted son and heir, and Mark Antony, one of Caesar's generals. In 42 BC, Octavian and Antony joined forces and divided Rome's territory between them. Antony took the eastern part, including Egypt, where he and Cleopatra began to build a vast empire.

EUROPE

AFRICA

KEY TO MAP

OCTAVIAN'S PROVINCES

ANTONY'S PROVINCES AND CLIENT STATES

GAUL (FRANCE)

ITALY

ADRIATIC SEA

THE BALKANS

TERRITORY FOR ALEXANDER HELIOS

• Artaxarta

ARMENIA

Rome •

SARDINIA

Brindisi •

• Philippi

MACEDONIA

Phraaspa •

MEDIA

Corfu • • Pharsalus

ASIA

CILICIA

SYRIA

SICILY

Actium •

• Ephesus

Tarsus •

TERRITORY FOR PTOLEMY PHILADELPHUS

IONIAN SEA

Patrae • Athens

Samos

• Antioch

ACHEA (GREECE)

• Cape Taenarum

PHOENICIA

MEDITERRANEAN SEA

• Ascalon

JUDEA

N

Alexandria •

• Pelusium

W — E

TERRITORY FOR CLEOPATRA SELENE

River Nile

TERRITORY FOR QUEEN CLEOPATRA AND PTOLEMY XV (CAESARION)

EGYPT

S

Hermonthis •

LAND OF THE PHARAOHS

*T*hroughout their dynasty, the Ptolemies held onto their Greek culture and continued to speak Greek as their main language. However, they used the title of pharaoh, the traditional and all-powerful ruler of Egypt.

RULERS OF EGYPT

The Ancient Egyptians believed that their kings were related to Ra, the sun god. They were also thought to be closely connected to Horus, the falcon god. The kings were given the title 'pharaoh' which means 'great house'. The pharaohs had absolute power. They directed the government, foreign policy and trade. They made laws, led the army into battle and were responsible for the harvest.

A statue of an Egyptian pharaoh, dressed in royal clothing.

THE PTOLEMIES

The founder of the Ptolemaic dynasty, Ptolemy I (ruled 305-284 BC), was followed by 15 kings of the same name. The dynasty also included seven queens who were rulers too. The Ptolemies were originally from Macedonia, in modern day Greece. The Ptolemies preserved their Greek culture and introduced many Greek customs to Egypt. They also introduced the custom of marrying their close relatives. Ptolemy II married his sister, Arsinoe II, and this practice continued for years. The last of the Ptolemies was Cleopatra VII. When she committed suicide in 30 BC, the dynasty died out.

An ancient bust of Ptolemy I.
A general in Alexander's army, he became governor, then king of Egypt.

OSIRIS   ISIS   HORUS

GODS ON EARTH
At the time of the Ptolemies, many Greek gods were joined with the Egyptian gods. The Ptolemaic kings followed Egyptian custom and worshipped the Egyptian god, Osiris. Cleopatra saw herself as Osiris's wife and sister, Isis. She likened her son, Caesarion, to Horus, the son of Osiris and Isis.

THE QUEEN OF KINGS

Cleopatra VII became queen when her father, Ptolemy XII, or Auletes, died in 51 BC. According to Ptolemaic custom, she ruled jointly with her half brothers, Ptolemy XIII and Ptolemy XIV, then with her son, Ptolemy XV, or Caesarion. Intelligent, charming, and determined, Cleopatra was a strong ruler. She was set on trying to achieve her greatest ambition – restoring the glory of the Ptolemaic dynasty. She was helped by her relationships with Romans Julius Caesar and Mark Antony.

A carving of Cleopatra dressed as Isis, the Egyptian goddess. She wears Isis's emblem, the snake, on her forehead. In Egyptian myth, Isis and her husband, Osiris, once ruled Egypt.

CLEOPATRA
THE LIFE OF AN EGYPTIAN QUEEN

THE ROYAL PALACE OF PTOLEMY XII IN ALEXANDRIA, EGYPT – 58 BC...

DOWN WITH AULETES!

STORM THE PALACE!

THE PEOPLE ARE AT THE GATES, SIRE. WE MUST LEAVE **NOW!**

WHERE ARE CLEOPATRA AND ARSINOE, MY TWO DAUGHTERS?

ALREADY ON BOARD THE SHIP.

PROTARCHUS, TELL THE MOB THAT I'VE **FLED**. THAT SHOULD CALM THEM DOWN.

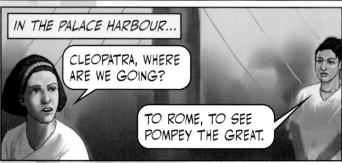

IN THE PALACE HARBOUR...

CLEOPATRA, WHERE ARE WE GOING?

TO ROME, TO SEE POMPEY THE GREAT.

HASN'T OUR FATHER GIVEN THAT ROMAN ENOUGH MONEY?

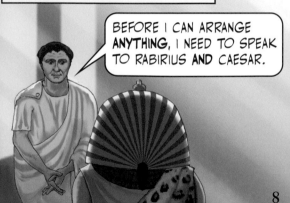

SIX WEEKS LATER, THEY REACH POMPEY'S VILLA IN ROME...

BEFORE I CAN ARRANGE **ANYTHING**, I NEED TO SPEAK TO RABIRIUS **AND** CAESAR.

TWO YEARS EARLIER, WHEN HIS RULE WAS IN TROUBLE, THE EGYPTIAN KING, PTOLEMY XII OR AULETES HAD ASKED THE ROMANS FOR HELP. POMPEY AND THEN CONSUL, JULIUS CAESAR, AGREED TO GET ROMAN SUPPORT FOR THE KING IN THE SENATE. BUT IT CAME AT A **HIGH PRICE**. AULETES COULD NOT RISK ANGERING HIS PEOPLE BY TAXING THEM, SO HE BORROWED MONEY FROM THE POWERFUL ROMAN BUSINESSMAN, *RABIRIUS*.

POMPEY SUMMONS RABIRIUS...

POMPEY, I STILL HAVEN'T BEEN **PAID**. AND IF YOU DON'T HELP AULETES, I NEVER WILL BE!

MEANWHILE, IN AULETES'S QUARTERS...

SIRE, YOUR ENEMIES HAVE MADE YOUR ELDEST DAUGHTER, BERENICE, QUEEN OF EGYPT.

POMPEY CALLS FOR AULETES.

CAESAR HAS GENEROUSLY AGREED TO ACCEPT RESPONSIBILITY FOR YOUR DEBT TO RABIRIUS.

AND AULUS GABINIUS, THE GOVERNOR OF SYRIA, WILL LEAD AN ARMY INTO EGYPT TO PLACE YOU BACK ON YOUR THRONE.

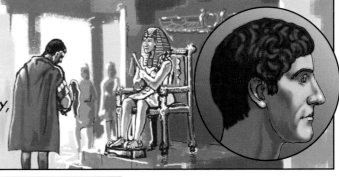

THE PRICE FOR THIS SUPPORT WAS DOUBLE WHAT IT WAS BEFORE. BUT AULETES ACCEPTED THE DEAL. THE FOLLOWING YEAR, GABINIUS'S LEGIONS, LED BY THE YOUNG CAVALRY OFFICER, **MARK ANTONY**, OVERCAME LOCAL FORCES TO PLACE KING PTOLEMY XII BACK ON HIS THRONE.

AULETES QUICKLY HAS BERENICE PUT TO DEATH. NOW CLEOPATRA IS THE OLDEST DAUGHTER. HER SISTER, **ARSINOE**, IS HORRIFIED.

IT WAS **WRONG** OF FATHER TO KILL HER!

NO! SHE WAS DISLOYAL. WE **NEED** THE ROMANS TO HELP US. YOU SHOULD **KNOW** THAT.

FOR OVER **300 YEARS**, AULETES'S ANCESTORS, THE PTOLEMIES, HAVE RULED EGYPT ALONE. NOW **CLEOPATRA**, HER FATHER'S FAVOURITE AND HIS GREATEST SUPPORTER, IS HIS HOPE FOR **THE FUTURE**.

SEVEN YEARS LATER, IN ALEXANDRIA...

THE KING IS DEAD!

AT 18 YEARS OLD, CLEOPATRA IS TO BECOME **QUEEN**. BUT UNDER EGYPTIAN LAW, A QUEEN CANNOT RULE WITHOUT A **KING**. IN HIS WILL, AULETES HAD NAMED THE ELDEST OF HIS TWO SONS, AND CLEOPATRA'S HALF BROTHER, TO BECOME **PTOLEMY XIII** AND RULE AT HER SIDE.

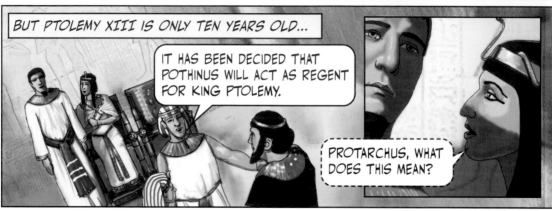

BUT PTOLEMY XIII IS ONLY TEN YEARS OLD...

IT HAS BEEN DECIDED THAT POTHINUS WILL ACT AS REGENT FOR KING PTOLEMY.

PROTARCHUS, WHAT DOES THIS MEAN?

PROTARCHUS HAS BECOME PRIME MINISTER AND IS NOW QUEEN CLEOPATRA'S CHIEF ADVISER.

YOUR MAJESTY, IT MEANS THAT POTHINUS **COULD** OVERRULE **ANY** OF YOUR DECISIONS, IN THE INTERESTS OF THE KING.

THAT'S **NOT** WHAT MY FATHER WANTED.

WE MUST SEE THAT IT DOES **NOT** HAPPEN.

CLEOPATRA BEGINS TO GATHER SUPPORT AGAINST HER HALF BROTHER. BUT IN 51 BC, TROUBLE BEGINS WITH THE ARMY. THE ARMY IS MAINLY MADE UP OF GABINIUS'S TROOPS WHO HAVE STAYED IN EGYPT TO SERVE AS MERCENARIES FOR THE RULERS OF EGYPT.

THE ROMAN GOVERNOR OF SYRIA, BIBULUS, HAS SENT HIS SONS TO SEEK HELP FROM CLEOPATRA'S 'GABINIANS' IN GUARDING HIS BORDERS...

AND EXACTLY **WHY** IS THIS A PROBLEM, PROTARCHUS?

BECAUSE THE GABINIANS HAVE MURDERED THEM BOTH, YOUR MAJESTY.

I SEE.

HAVE THE MEN RESPONSIBLE ARRESTED AND SENT TO BIBULUS IN **CHAINS** – WITH MY BEST WISHES.

THIS ACTION **STIRS UP** THE ANTI-ROMAN FEELINGS OF THE PEOPLE OF ALEXANDRIA. CLEOPATRA NOW FINDS EVERY DECISION SHE MAKES BEING OVERRULED BY POTHINUS. TO MAKE MATTERS WORSE, THE HARVEST HAS FAILED. THERE IS WIDESPREAD UNREST UP AND DOWN THE COUNTRY AS PEOPLE START TO GO HUNGRY.

A FEW MONTHS LATER, BAD NEWS COMES FROM ACROSS THE MEDITERRANEAN SEA...

ROME IS AT WAR!

...WITH HERSELF!

TROUBLE HAS ERUPTED BETWEEN POMPEY THE GREAT AND HIS FORMER ALLY, JULIUS CAESAR, THE CONQUEROR OF GAUL. IT ENDS WITH CAESAR BRINGING HIS TROOPS BACK FROM GAUL TO MARCH ON ROME. BEFORE LONG, ROME IS DIVIDED BY A BLOODY **CIVIL WAR**.

IN EGYPT...

IT IS NO LONGER SAFE FOR YOU TO STAY HERE, YOUR MAJESTY.

WHERE SHALL I GO?

YOU SHOULD GO TO **ASCALON**. YOU HAVE ALLIES THERE.

CLEOPATRA TRAVELS EAST TO THE CITY OF ASCALON IN JUDEA. MEANWHILE, POMPEY AND **HIS** SUPPORTERS ARE BUSY LEAVING ROME TO SET UP A BASE OF OPERATIONS IN THE BALKANS. IN EARLY 49 BC, POMPEY SENDS HIS SON, CNAEUS, TO ALEXANDRIA WITH A SPECIAL REQUEST.

HAVE NO DOUBT WE **WILL** DEFEAT THE TYRANT CAESAR. BUT WE NEED EXTRA SHIPS AND MEN. WILL YOU HELP US?

POTHINUS SPEAKS FOR THE KING...

WE WILL GIVE YOU 60 SHIPS AND A COHORT OF OUR FINEST GABINIAN SOLDIERS.

LATER...

I SUGGEST WE ACCOMPANY THE REST OF THE ARMY TO THE BORDER TO DEAL WITH YOUR SISTER **FOR GOOD**.

SOON, ALL EYES TURN TOWARD THE BALKANS. IN AUGUST 48 BC, THE TWO GREAT ARMIES OF POMPEY AND CAESAR MEET AT PHARSALUS TO FIGHT THE DECISIVE BATTLE OF THE ROMAN CIVIL WAR.

CAESAR IS A BRILLIANT GENERAL AND HE PROVES IT AGAIN WITH A GREAT VICTORY. HE DRIVES POMPEY'S FORCES BACK THROUGH THEIR OWN CAMP. POMPEY HIMSELF ESCAPES BY SEA TO EGYPT. HE THEN SENDS A MESSENGER TO ASK FOR A MEETING WITH KING PTOLEMY.

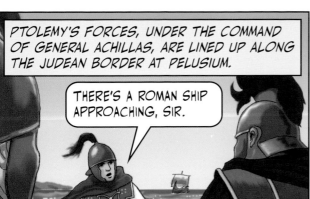

PTOLEMY'S FORCES, UNDER THE COMMAND OF GENERAL ACHILLAS, ARE LINED UP ALONG THE JUDEAN BORDER AT PELUSIUM.

THERE'S A ROMAN SHIP APPROACHING, SIR.

ACHILLAS, DO YOU THINK IT COULD BE...

POMPEY? YES, GET MY BOAT READY. I HAVE ORDERS TO DEAL WITH THIS **PERSONALLY**.

FOUR DAYS LATER, AT THE TOP OF THE PHAROS LIGHTHOUSE IN ALEXANDRIA HARBOUR...

TELL THE REGENT THERE ARE ROMAN **SHIPS** APPROACHING!

IT IS CAESAR!

THE COURT CHAMBERLAIN, THEODOTUS, LEADS THE EGYPTIANS TO GREET CAESAR...

WELCOME, GREAT CAESAR! THE KING HAS SENT A GIFT FOR YOU...

...THE HEAD OF POMPEY THE GREAT!

BARBARIANS!

FIND THE **REST** OF POMPEY, WHATEVER IT TAKES.

13

THEODOTUS CONTINUES...

OF COURSE, WE ARE HAPPY TO PROVIDE YOU WITH WHATEVER YOU NEED BEFORE YOU LEAVE.

 LEAVING? OH NO, NO ONE'S **LEAVING.**

 NOT UNTIL I'VE SOLVED THIS QUARREL BETWEEN YOUR TWO RULERS.

AND I ALSO HAVE A **DEBT** TO COLLECT.

CAESAR NEEDS THE MONEY THAT PTOLEMY'S LATE FATHER, AULETES, STILL OWES HIM. HE NEEDS TO PAY OFF HIS SOLDIERS AND HIRE NEW ONES FOR THE COMING BATTLE AGAINST POMPEY'S SONS. HE IS GIVEN ROOMS IN THE ROYAL PALACE. BUT RATHER THAN ENTER THE CITY DRESSED AS A GENERAL, CAESAR WEARS HIS CONSUL'S TOGA AND MARCHES IN FULL GLORY.

THE ALEXANDRIANS BECOME FURIOUS AT THE ROMAN GENERAL...

THE MOB KILLED SEVERAL OF OUR GUARDS, CAESAR!

SEND FOR MORE SHIPS AND MEN. WE MAY NEED THEM.

CAESAR THEN SENDS MESSAGES TO PTOLEMY AND CLEOPATRA TO COME FOR TALKS AT THE ROYAL PALACE. A FEW WEEKS LATER, THE REQUEST REACHES THE QUEEN AT MOUNT CASSIUS WHERE SHE IS TRAPPED BY ACHILLAS'S FORCES.

YOUR MAJESTY, YOU CANNOT GO!

AS SOON AS YOU SHOW YOURSELF, POTHINUS WILL HAVE YOU **KILLED!**

BUT I **NEED** TO SPEAK TO CAESAR. THERE **MUST** BE A WAY...

THREE WEEKS LATER, IN THE PALACE HARBOUR...

WHO GOES THERE?

I HAVE A GIFT FOR CAESAR FROM QUEEN CLEOPATRA!

THIS WAY.

A GIFT? VERY WELL, JUST LEAVE IT IN THE CORNER.

?

WOOOOOSH!

PLOP!

QUEEN CLEOPATRA?

I BEG YOU TO PROTECT ME, CAESAR. MY LIFE IS IN DANGER.

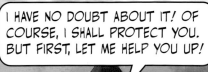

I HAVE NO DOUBT ABOUT IT! OF COURSE, I SHALL PROTECT YOU. BUT FIRST, LET ME HELP YOU UP!

15

WITH CAESAR TO PROTECT HER, CLEOPATRA APPEARS BEFORE THE ROYAL COURT. KING PTOLEMY IS FURIOUS.

POTHINUS! WHAT'S **SHE** DOING HERE?

TRAITOR!

AFTER HIM!

OUTSIDE THE PALACE GATES...

GRAB HIM!

HELP ME! THEY WANT TO TAKE AWAY MY THRONE!

CAESAR'S TROOPS DRAG THE 13-YEAR-OLD KING BACK INSIDE.

LATER...

I WANT TO GET RID OF HER, POTHINUS!

YOUR MAJESTY, THE QUEEN AND CAESAR HAVE BECOME VERY...**CLOSE**.

WE CANNOT GET TO **HER** WITHOUT GETTING RID OF **HIM**. TO DO THIS, WE WOULD NEED THE SUPPORT OF ACHILLAS AND THE ARMY.

CAESAR URGES CLEOPATRA AND PTOLEMY TO MAKE PEACE. THEN, TO CALM THE ANGRY ALEXANDRIANS, HE GIVES THE ISLAND OF CYPRUS, PREVIOUSLY SEIZED BY THE ROMANS, BACK TO THE EGYPTIANS BY PRESENTING IT TO CLEOPATRA'S SISTER, ARSINOE.

WELL THEN, **GET** THEM HERE!

AS YOU WISH.

16

SO TELL ME, WHY IS EGYPTIAN WINE SO SUPERIOR TO ROMAN?

BANG! BANG! BANG!

SIR! GUARDS REPORT THAT ACHILLAS AND THE GABINIAN ARMY ARE MARCHING ON THE PALACE!

RALLY THE TROOPS, SEAL THE PALACE, AND PLACE THE KING UNDER GUARD.

LATER...

THAT SHOULD HOLD THEM, FOR A WHILE.

COMMANDER, COME QUICKLY!

IT'S THE EGYPTIAN NAVY. WE ARE SURROUNDED!

WAIT FOR ME IN MY QUARTERS, MY DARLING. I WON'T BE LONG.

CLEOPATRA WATCHES AS CAESAR AND HIS MEN CAPTURE THE EGYPTIAN SHIPS, ONE BY ONE. THEN CAESAR ORDERS ALL THE SHIPS SET ON FIRE.

CAESAR THEN SENDS SOLDIERS TO CAPTURE THE PHAROS LIGHTHOUSE. THIS MAKES THE HARBOUR SECURE FOR SHIPS AND REINFORCEMENTS TO ARRIVE FROM ROME.

IN CAESAR'S QUARTERS, CLEOPATRA WAITS WITH HER MAID...

SHALL I PREPARE A VICTORY BATH FOR THE COMMANDER?

NO CELEBRATIONS YET. ACHILLAS STILL HAS US UNDER SIEGE, AND HE HAS **THE MOB** ON HIS SIDE.

CAESAR! THANK RA!

THEN...

YOUR MAJESTY, IT SEEMS THAT ARSINOE AND HER ADVISER, GANYMEDES, HAVE ESCAPED TO JOIN ACHILLAS.

A FEW DAYS LATER...

I HAVE HEARD THAT GANYMEDES AND ACHILLAS HAVE BEGUN **FIGHTING** OVER WHO SHOULD TAKE COMMAND.

THEN...

THIS IS POTHINUS'S BARBER, SIR. HE WANTS TO TELL YOU SOMETHING.

MY MASTER HAS BEEN SENDING SECRET MESSAGES OF SUPPORT TO GENERAL ACHILLAS!

I THINK IT'S TIME WE SENT FOR REINFORCEMENTS.

AND POTHINUS?

KILL HIM!

THE FOLLOWING DAY...

IT SEEMS THE MOB HAS CHOSEN A NEW COMMANDER.

GANYMEDES HOLDS UP THE HEAD OF ACHILLAS...

SO – WE HAVE A **NEW** ENEMY!

WITHIN A FEW DAYS, THE EXTRA SHIPS THAT CAESAR ORDERED SIX WEEKS EARLIER ARRIVE IN THE HARBOUR. ON THE ROOF OF THE PALACE, HE OUTLINES HIS NEXT MOVE...

AFTER CAPTURING PHAROS ISLAND, I WILL LEAD A GROUP OF MEN TO CAPTURE THE MOLE AND BARRICADE IT FROM THE CITY.*

*THE MOLE WAS THE CAUSEWAY LINKING PHAROS ISLAND TO THE MAINLAND.

THE ROMANS TAKE THE MOLE AND START TO BUILD THE BARRICADE. BUT THEN CLEOPATRA WATCHES IN HORROR AS EGYPTIAN TROOPS LAND BEHIND THEM, CUTTING CAESAR'S SOLDIERS OFF.

THEN...

OH NO! LOOK AT THE COMMANDER'S SHIP. IT'S SINKING!

AS THE EGYPTIANS ARRIVE, THE ROMANS BEGIN TO MOVE THEIR SHIPS AWAY. THE ROMAN SOLDIERS PANIC AND TRY TO FORCE THEIR WAY ON BOARD THE MOVING SHIPS.

AS CAESAR'S SHIP BECOMES OVERLOADED, IT TIPS OVER AND **SINKS** WITH EVERYONE ON BOARD.

LATER...

CAESAR!

RA BE PRAISED!

THAT WAS A LUCKY ESCAPE, I'LL ADMIT!

FOR SEVERAL WEEKS LONGER, THE CITY REMAINS UNDER SIEGE. GANYMEDES COMMANDS THE ARMY ON BEHALF OF PTOLEMY. THEN, AT LAST, NEWS COMES THAT A ROMAN RELIEF FORCE IS APPROACHING THE CITY FROM THE SOUTH. LEAVING BEHIND A SMALL GROUP OF MEN TO GUARD THE QUEEN, CAESAR DECIDES TO BREAK OUT OF THE PALACE AND JOIN THEM.

I **WILL** RETURN SAFELY, YOUR MAJESTY. I **PROMISE.**

CAESAR TAKES COMMAND OF THE RELIEF FORCE AND FIGHTS PTOLEMY BY LAKE MAREOTIS, JUST OUTSIDE ALEXANDRIA. THE ROMANS QUICKLY CRUSH THE EGYPTIAN ARMY. SOON CAESAR IS PARADING THROUGH THE CITY TO THE ROYAL PALACE – THE CROWD CHEER THE VICTORIOUS COMMANDER.

MAGNIFICENT!

I ALWAYS KEEP MY PROMISES!

GANYMEDES AND THE GABINIANS HAVE BEEN **KILLED.** KING PTOLEMY WAS ALSO REPORTED DEAD, BUT HIS **BODY** WAS NOT FOUND.

WE **HAVE** TO FIND HIM. ORGANISE A SEARCH!

CLEOPATRA HAS TO BE SURE. SHE CANNOT TAKE THE RISK THAT PTOLEMY MIGHT STILL BE ALIVE AND MAY, ONE DAY, COME BACK TO CHALLENGE HER.

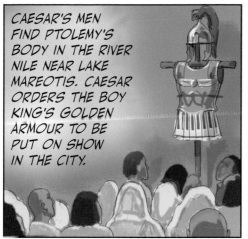

CAESAR'S MEN FIND PTOLEMY'S BODY IN THE RIVER NILE NEAR LAKE MAREOTIS. CAESAR ORDERS THE BOY KING'S GOLDEN ARMOUR TO BE PUT ON SHOW IN THE CITY.

THEN CAESAR SUMMONS HIS TRUSTED SERVANT, THE FORMER SLAVE, **RUFIO**.

I INTEND TO LEAVE THREE LEGIONS BEHIND TO SUPPORT THE QUEEN. I AM PUTTING YOU IN CHARGE OF THEM, RUFIO.

WILL YOU RETURN TO ROME, SIR?

I WILL, SOON.

CAESAR ACCEPTS THE QUEEN'S INVITATION TO JOIN HER ON THE ROYAL BARGE, LEADING A FLOTILLA OF OVER 400 CRAFT UP THE RIVER NILE.

THE PROCESSION IS MEANT TO BE A DISPLAY OF CLEOPATRA'S POWER. SHE AND CAESAR MAKE TIME TO VISIT A TEMPLE...

COME AND MEET MY ANCESTORS.

AMONG THE GODS OF EGYPT, OSIRIS AND ISIS, EGYPT'S KING AND QUEEN, ARE ESPECIALLY IMPORTANT TO THE ROYAL FAMILY.

IF YOUR **OSIRIS** IS OUR ROMAN GOD, **DIONYSUS**, AND YOUR **ISIS** IS OUR **VENUS**, THAT LITTLE FIGURE THERE MUST BE...

THEIR SON, OUR HORUS!

IN 47 BC, CLEOPATRA GIVES BIRTH TO A SON, NAMED PTOLEMY CAESAR.*

*ALSO KNOWN AS CAESARION.

SHE ALSO HONOURS HER GREAT ROMAN PROTECTOR WITH A NEW BUILDING ON THE ALEXANDRIAN WATERFRONT, THE CAESAREUM.

CAESAR HIMSELF IS FINALLY BACK IN ROME. AFTER SUCCESSFUL CAMPAIGNS IN ASIA AND AFRICA, THE SENATE MAKES HIM DICTATOR FOR 10 MORE YEARS. CAESAR CELEBRATES HIS VICTORIES. AMONG HIS MANY PRISONERS OF WAR IS CLEOPATRA'S SISTER, ARSINOE. SHE HAS BEEN TAKEN CAPTIVE AFTER THE WAR IN ALEXANDRIA.

BACK IN EGYPT, CLEOPATRA IS RESTLESS...

THINGS ARE SO QUIET HERE. I HOPE HE HASN'T FORGOTTEN ABOUT ME.

PERHAPS A STATE VISIT IS IN ORDER?

CLEOPATRA SENDS WORD TO CAESAR OF HER WISH TO VISIT ROME. CAESAR OFFERS HER HIS FINEST ROMAN VILLA FOR HER STAY IN THE CITY.

SOME TIME LATER, CLEOPATRA ARRIVES IN ROME. SHE IS ACCOMPANIED BY HER NEW CO-RULER AND YOUNGEST HALF BROTHER, PTOLEMY XIV, AND HER SON. LARGE CROWDS FLOCK TO WATCH HER ARRIVAL...

CAESAR ARRANGES A MEETING IN HIS NEW TEMPLE. IT IS DEDICATED TO **VENUS, GODDESS OF LOVE.**

I HAVE SOMETHING TO SHOW YOU.

I THINK IT IS ONLY FITTING THAT **ISIS** AND **HORUS** SHOULD STAND HERE IN THIS TEMPLE, WITH **VENUS.**

THE STATUE IS A GREAT HONOUR FOR CLEOPATRA AND CAESARION.

LESS THAN 18 MONTHS LATER, CAESAR IS DEAD. HE HAD MADE HIMSELF DICTATOR FOR LIFE AND ACTED AS THOUGH HE WAS KING. THE SENATE FELT THREATENED BY HIS GROWING POWER. ON 15TH MARCH, 44 BC, A GROUP OF ANGRY SENATORS, LED BY BRUTUS AND CASSIUS, AMBUSHED CAESAR AND STABBED HIM TO DEATH.

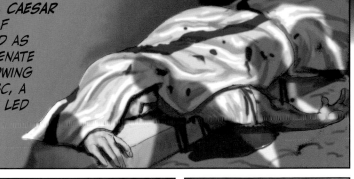

TWO DAYS LATER, CAESAR'S WILL IS READ. BUT THERE IS NO MENTION OF CAESARION...

CAESAR WISHES HIS GREAT NEPHEW AND ADOPTED SON, OCTAVIAN, TO BE HIS SOLE HEIR.

FROM HIS BASE ON THE ISLAND OF RHODES, **OCTAVIAN** QUICKLY SIGNALS TO THE SENATE THAT HE FULLY INTENDS TO **CLAIM** HIS INHERITANCE. SHORTLY AFTERWARDS, CLEOPATRA AND HER COMPANIONS LEAVE ROME AND TRAVEL BACK TO EGYPT.

BACK IN EGYPT, CLEOPATRA SUMMONS PROTARCHUS...

I AM WORRIED ABOUT CAESARION'S **FUTURE.**

I THINK IT WOULD BE SAFER FOR HIM IF HE WERE MADE KING.

YES, BUT THAT'S NOT POSSIBLE WHILE YOUR HALF BROTHER IS...

STILL ALIVE?

THEIR RELATIONSHIP BECOMES THE TALK OF TARSUS.

IT'S AS IF THE GODS OF LOVE ARE SMILING DOWN ON THE TWO OF THEM!

BUT THERE IS ALSO SOME HARD BARGAINING TO BE DONE...

EGYPT WILL OFFER YOU ALL THE HELP YOU NEED FOR YOUR WAR, ON TWO CONDITIONS.

NAME THEM.

MY SISTER, ARSINOE, IS IN EXILE IN EPHESUS.

I WANT HER KILLED.

AND THERE IS A YOUTH IN PHOENICIA WHO CLAIMS TO BE MY YOUNGER BROTHER.* KILL HIM, TOO.

*PTOLEMY XIII, WHO HAD DROWNED.

CONSIDER IT DONE.

ANTONY IS CHARMED BY THE QUEEN. HE AGREES TO SPEND THE WINTER AS HER GUEST AT THE ROYAL PALACE. NOT ONLY IS CLEOPATRA YOUNG, BEAUTIFUL, AND RICH, SHE IS ALSO CLEVER – UNLIKE HIS WIFE, FULVIA, IN ROME.

FULVIA HAS JOINED FORCES WITH ANTONY'S BROTHER, LUCIUS, IN A PLOT TO **OVERTHROW** OCTAVIAN.

ANTONY KNOWS NOTHING ABOUT THIS. HE IS ENJOYING THE MANY DELIGHTS AND LUXURIES OF CLEOPATRA'S ROYAL PALACE.

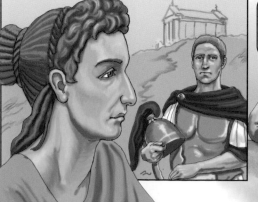

QUINTUS, HAVE YOU EVER KNOWN SUCH FOOD, SUCH WINE, OR SUCH DELIGHTFUL ENTERTAINMENT?

THEN...

LORD ANTONY, I HAVE SERIOUS NEWS!

THE PARTHIANS HAVE INVADED SYRIA!

THIS IS A BLOW. HE HAS NOT INTENDED TO ATTACK THE PARTHIANS UNTIL SPRING.

LATER, ANTONY PREPARES TO LEAVE. HE SAYS FAREWELL TO CLEOPATRA...

GOOD LUCK, AND COME BACK AS SOON AS YOU CAN.

WE WILL BE HERE FOR YOU...**ALL OF US.**

SHE IS PREGNANT.

ANTONY SETS SAIL FOR THE CITY OF TYRE IN THE MIDDLE EAST. AMONG HIS BAND OF COMPANIONS IS AN ASTROLOGER FROM EGYPT. HE HAS BEEN SENT BY CLEOPATRA WITH STRICT INSTRUCTIONS TO SEND HER REGULAR REPORTS OF ANTONY'S MOVEMENTS.

THREE WEEKS LATER, THE FIRST REPORT ARRIVES...

"WE WERE FOUR DAYS OUT OF ALEXANDRIA WHEN WORD CAME THAT LORD ANTONY'S WIFE, FULVIA, HAD BEEN WORKING IN LEAGUE WITH HIS BROTHER. SHE SEEMS TO HAVE BEEN DEFEATED BY OCTAVIAN IN BATTLE AND HAS FLED TO GREECE, WHICH IS WHERE WE ARE NOW HEADING."

ATHENS, GREECE – EARLY 40 BC...

WHY, FULVIA? WHY?

PLEASE, ANTONY! I ONLY DID IT FOR YOU!

YOU ARE IN DANGER FROM OCTAVIAN. I WAS TRYING TO HELP YOU!

HELP ME! YOU HAVE ONLY HARMED ME, WOMAN! NOW, GET OUT OF MY SIGHT.

ANTONY CHARGES OUT OF ATHENS READY TO FACE OCTAVIAN, AND THEN THE PARTHIANS. FULVIA STAYS BEHIND BUT DIES A FEW MONTHS LATER.

OVER THE NEXT YEAR, CLEOPATRA CONTINUES TO RECEIVE REPORTS OF ANTONY'S TROUBLES...

HIS TROOPS IN SYRIA HAVE LEFT HIM!

AND SUCCESSES...

HE HAS DRIVEN THE PARTHIANS FROM SYRIA!

IN LATE 40 BC, CLEOPATRA GIVES BIRTH TO ANTONY'S TWINS – A GIRL, CLEOPATRA, AND A BOY, ALEXANDER.

WILL YOU BE A LEGEND LIKE YOUR NAMESAKE, ALEXANDER THE GREAT, OR INDEED, YOUR FATHER?

IF HE MANAGES TO BEAT THE PARTHIANS, AND THEN...OCTAVIAN!

BUT DISTURBING NEWS ARRIVES...

"WE ARE IN BRINDISI TO ARRANGE A TREATY BETWEEN LORD ANTONY AND OCTAVIAN. IT HAS BEEN SEALED BY THE MARRIAGE OF ANTONY TO OCTAVIAN'S SISTER, OCTAVIA. BY ALL ACCOUNTS, SHE IS A WOMAN OF GREAT BEAUTY, GRACE, AND REFINEMENT."

PROTARCHUS, IS OCTAVIA REALLY THIS WONDERFUL?

I DON'T KNOW, BUT I HAVE HEARD THAT THE WHOLE ROMAN WORLD IS HAPPY ABOUT THEIR MARRIAGE.

THE ROMAN WORLD IS HAPPY THAT OCTAVIAN AND ANTONY HAVE MADE PEACE. ANTONY AND HIS NEW WIFE ARE A MODEL COUPLE. THEY MAKE THEIR BASE IN ATHENS. FROM HERE, ANTONY MAKES PLANS TO WAGE WAR ON PARTHIA. HE SAILS EAST IN AUTUMN 37 BC, WITH OCTAVIA BY HIS SIDE.

THE COUPLE TRAVEL AS FAR AS THE ISLAND OF CORFU. ANTONY IS WORRIED.

I DON'T THINK YOU SHOULD COME WITH ME.

THE ROUTE TO SYRIA CAN BE RISKY AT THIS TIME OF YEAR. YOU WILL BE MUCH SAFER IN ROME, MY LOVE.

FOUR WEEKS LATER IN ANTIOCH, SYRIA...

CLEOPATRA, HOW I HAVE LONGED FOR THIS MOMENT EVER SINCE WE PARTED.

EVEN ON YOUR **WEDDING DAY?**

ANTONY, THE ONLY REASON YOU ARE HERE IS TO ASK FOR MY HELP WITH YOUR WAR.

NOT TRUE! I AM **ALSO** HERE TO ASK FOR YOUR **LOVE!**

CLEOPATRA IS WILLING TO GIVE IT, **AND** THE HELP HE NEEDS. BUT THERE **ARE** CONDITIONS...

THERE ARE CERTAIN TERRITORIES THAT BELONGED TO MY ANCESTOR, PTOLEMY II. NOW I WANT THEM BACK.

AND THEN TAKE PARTHIA...

IF YOU GIVE ME THESE LANDS...

WE COULD BUILD AN EMPIRE THAT WOULD BE EVEN BIGGER THAN **ALEXANDER'S!**

CLEOPATRA DRIVES A HARD BARGAIN BUT ANTONY AGREES TO HER CONDITIONS. HE GIVES HER BACK HER LOST LANDS. HER KINGDOM IS NOW FAR BIGGER THAN BEFORE.

IN RETURN, CLEOPATRA WILL PROVIDE SOLDIERS. SHE WILL ALSO USE TIMBER FROM HER RETURNED LANDS TO BUILD SHIPS TO PROTECT ANTONY'S ARMY DURING HIS INVASION OF PARTHIA. THIS IS DUE TO BEGIN THE FOLLOWING MAY.

SEVEN MONTHS LATER IN SYRIA, ANTONY IS FINALLY READY TO BEGIN HIS WAR.

WE WILL MARCH INTO ARMENIA AND THEN TAKE MEDIA.

MONAESES, OUR NEW ALLY, WILL HELP US.

A PARTHIAN LEADER, MONAESES HAS COME OVER TO ANTONY'S SIDE.

THE **ARMENIAN** RULER, ARTAVASDES, GIVES IN EASILY. HE EVEN ACCOMPANIES ANTONY'S ARMY INTO MEDIA.

BUT THE MARCH IS TAKING TOO LONG. ANTONY NEEDS TO REACH THE MEDIAN CAPITAL, PHRAASPA, BEFORE AUTUMN.

WE WILL SPLIT THE ARMY. THE BAGGAGE TRAIN WILL FOLLOW BEHIND, GUARDED BY TWO LEGIONS.

THIS PROVES TO BE A BAD MISTAKE. THE BAGGAGE TRAIN COMES UNDER ATTACK FROM MONAESES WHO NOW TURNS AGAINST ANTONY. ALL ANTONY'S SOLDIERS ARE KILLED AND HIS EQUIPMENT SET ON FIRE. MEANWHILE, ARTAVASDES AND THE ARMENIANS RUN AWAY.

AT PHRAASPA, ANTONY IS POWERLESS.

WITHOUT HIS SIEGE EQUIPMENT, HE CANNOT TAKE THE CITY. ANTONY TURNS BACK TO SYRIA, PESTERED BY THE PARTHIAN CAVALRY AND THE WORSENING WEATHER. ANTONY HAS LOST 28,000 MEN AND GAINED NOTHING. PARTHIA WILL HOLD OUT FOR ANOTHER 150 YEARS.

MEANWHILE, FAR TO THE WEST IN SARDINIA, ANTONY'S RIVAL, OCTAVIAN, HAS HIS OWN MILITARY DIFFICULTIES.

THE LAST TIME I FOUGHT SEXTUS, I LOST HALF MY SHIPS.

FOR MONTHS, HE HAS BEEN BATTLING SEXTUS, SON OF POMPEY AND NOW PIRATE OF THE SEAS AROUND SICILY.

I NEED TO **WIN** THIS TIME, AGRIPPA!

WILL YOU BRING ME A VICTORY TOMORROW?

MARCUS VISPANUS AGRIPPA IS OCTAVIAN'S TRUSTED FRIEND AND ADMIRAL OF THE NAVY. HE IS TO LEAD THE FINAL BATTLE HIMSELF.

YES, CAESAR!

AGRIPPA IS A GREAT NAVAL COMMANDER WHO HAS TRAINED HIS MEN TO PERFECTION. HE ALSO HAS A NEW SECRET WEAPON – **THE HARPAX**, A GRAPPLING HOOK FIRED FROM A CATAPULT. ON THE DAY, AGRIPPA BEATS SEXTUS EASILY, THANKS TO HIS USE OF THE HARPAX AND SEXTUS'S OVERCONFIDENCE. OCTAVIAN HAS HIS VICTORY.

> I, **CAESAR**, AM THE ONLY MAN WHO CAN NOW TRULY UNITE ROME!

> AND **NOTHING** WILL STAND IN HIS WAY.

IN ALEXANDRIA, CLEOPATRA RECEIVES A MESSAGE...

> IT'S FROM ANTONY. HE WANTS ME TO MEET HIM IN PHOENICIA WITH MONEY AND EQUIPMENT.

> WILL YOU GO?

> HOW CAN I REFUSE?

SHE HAS JUST HAD HIS THIRD CHILD, PTOLEMY PHILADELPHUS.

IN ROME, OCTAVIAN WATCHES EVENTS IN THE EAST WITH GREAT INTEREST. HE HAS HIS OWN SLY PLAN...

> WE'LL SUGGEST THAT OCTAVIA HELPS OUT ANTONY, AS CLEOPATRA HAS DONE.

> BUT WE WILL GIVE HER JUST A HANDFUL OF SHIPS AND **NO** INFANTRY.*

*ANTONY HAS BEEN PROMISED TWO LEGIONS.

> HE WILL TAKE THIS AS AN INSULT AND TURN HER AWAY. THEN ALL ROME WILL **HATE** HIM FOR IT!

THE TRICK WORKS. WHEN OCTAVIA OFFERS TO BRING 72 SHIPS TO ANTONY, HE TURNS HER AWAY. EVEN THE SENATORS WHO SUPPORTED HIM ARE ANGERED AT HIS WRONGING OF SUCH A MODEL ROMAN WIFE.

ANTONY DOES NOT CARE. HE IS TOO BUSY PLANNING THE GROWTH OF HIS EMPIRE WITH CLEOPATRA. THEIR PLANNING FINALLY PAYS OFF IN 34 BC. ANTONY MARCHES INTO ARMENIA AND ACCEPTS THE SURRENDER OF ARTAVASDES.

IN THE AUTUMN OF 34 BC, ANTONY MARCHES VICTORIOUSLY THROUGH ALEXANDRIA. HE IS DRESSED AS DIONYSUS, THE GOD OF JOY.

HE ARRIVES AT THE TEMPLE OF SARAPIS...

HE GREETS HIS QUEEN...

VENUS?

WELCOME, DIONYSUS!

THREE DAYS LATER, THE GREAT CEREMONY OF DONATIONS IS HELD IN THE CITY. QUEEN CLEOPATRA APPEARS AS THE GODDESS ISIS.

CLEOPATRA AND ANTONY ARE SEATED ON GOLDEN THRONES. THEN ANTONY RISES AND PRESENTS CLEOPATRA AND HER CHILDREN WITH NEW LANDS AND TITLES. CLEOPATRA BECOMES SUPREME QUEEN OF KINGS.

ALEXANDER HELIOS IS MADE KING OF ARMENIA AND OVERLORD OF MEDIA AND PARTHIA.

CLEOPATRA SELENE, HIS TWIN SISTER, IS MADE QUEEN OF CYRENAICA, THE EAST OF LIBYA.

PTOLEMY PHILADELPHUS IS MADE KING OF ALL SYRIAN LANDS AND OVERLORD OF ASIA.

CAESARION IS KING OF KINGS – JOINT OVERLORD OF THE EGYPTIAN EMPIRE WITH HIS MOTHER.

AT A FEAST HELD AFTERWARDS, THE ROMAN CONSUL PLANCUS ENTERTAINS THE GUESTS. HE IS DRESSED AS A SEA GOD.

IT'S NO GOOD. I CAN'T SEEM TO GET A BITE!

LEAVE THE FISHING TO US POOR PHARAOHS! YOUR SPORT IS TO HUNT KINGDOMS AND CONTINENTS!

NEWS OF THE DONATIONS REACHES OCTAVIAN IN ROME...

THE **SENATE** WILL NOT BE **REJOICING** WHEN THEY HEAR ABOUT THE ROMAN LANDS ANTONY HAS GIVEN AWAY.

LET THEM ENJOY THEIR EGYPTIAN VICTORY, WHILE THEY CAN.

IN JANUARY 33 BC, OCTAVIAN IS MADE CONSUL. HE USES HIS POWER TO ATTACK ANTONY IN THE SENATE.

WHERE **IS** LORD ANTONY?

I'LL TELL YOU! HE'S WITH HIS **EGYPTIAN MISTRESS** – THE **REAL** COMMANDER OF THE EASTERN ARMY!

SHE WANTS TO BE QUEEN OF ROME!

ANTONY VOICES HIS WORRIES TO PLANCUS...

WHY ARE THEY AGAINST ME? I WILL SEND A LETTER TO ANSWER THE CHARGES!

THE LETTER IS NEVER READ OUT. AT THE END OF 33 BC, OCTAVIAN GIVES UP HIS POWERS TO BECOME A PRIVATE CITIZEN. HE WANTS ANTONY TO DO THE SAME.

PLANCUS VOICES THE SENATORS' CONCERNS...

THEY FEAR THE REPUBLIC IS **DEAD**. THEY THINK THERE WILL BE **WAR**.

IN FEBRUARY 32 BC, THE NEWLY APPOINTED CONSULS, WHO BOTH SUPPORT ANTONY, MAKE SPEECHES AGAINST THE ABSENT OCTAVIAN. TWO WEEKS LATER, HE APPEARS IN THE SENATE WITH HIS BODYGUARD.

THESE CHARGES ARE FALSE!

REST ASSURED, I WILL RETURN WITH PROOF. THEN THOSE WHO HAVE LIED ABOUT ME HAD BETTER BEWARE!

THE SENATORS WHO SUPPORT ANTONY ARE HORRIFIED AT OCTAVIAN'S THREATS. THE NEXT WEEK, 200 OF THEM PACK THEIR BAGS AND FLEE TO GREECE. THEY WANT TO BE NEAR ANTONY IF WAR BREAKS OUT.

IN ALEXANDRIA, PLANCUS IS HAVING DOUBTS...

ANTONY'S A GOOD MAN, TITIUS, AND CLEOPATRA HAS LONG BEEN MY FRIEND.

BUT IT'S NO LONGER A QUESTION OF LOYALTY.

IT'S SIMPLY WHO WILL WIN.

HE CHOOSES OCTAVIAN.

IN ROME, PLANCUS TELLS OCTAVIAN THAT ANTONY'S WILL IS KEPT IN THE TEMPLE OF VESTA.

OCTAVIAN DEMANDS TO SEE IT. HE IS REFUSED BUT TAKES IT BY FORCE.

HE BRINGS IT TO THE SENATE...

HE ALSO WISHES TO BE BURIED NOT IN ROME...

BUT IN ALEXANDRIA!

ROAR!

HE CLAIMS CAESARION IS CAESAR'S SON AND HE HAS LEFT VAST LEGACIES FOR HIS EGYPTIAN CHILDREN!

WITH CLEOPATRA'S HELP, ANTONY HAS GATHERED A HUGE FORCE. HE HAS 300 MERCHANT SHIPS, 500 WARSHIPS, AND AN ARMY OF OVER 100,000 MEN.

IF THEY CELEBRATE LIKE THIS TO PREPARE FOR WAR, WHAT WOULD THEY DO FOR A VICTORY?

AS ANTONY DEALS WITH AFFAIRS OF STATE, CLEOPATRA SENDS HIM LOVE LETTERS WRITTEN ON TABLETS OF PRECIOUS STONE. IN APRIL, THEY MOVE TO THE ISLAND OF SAMOS. THEY HOLD A GREAT FESTIVAL OF MUSIC, DANCING, AND THEATRE.

THEN, IN ATHENS, ANTONY OUTLINES HIS PLAN FOR WAR...

WE WILL SET UP BASES IN THE IONIAN SEA TO PROTECT OUR SUPPLY ROUTE TO EGYPT.

AND MAKE OCTAVIAN COME AS FAR FROM ROME AS POSSIBLE.

HE KNOWS TIME IS ON THEIR SIDE. OCTAVIAN IS SHORT OF MONEY

IN ROME, OCTAVIAN HAS DECIDED TO **TAX** THE PEOPLE TO RAISE MONEY FOR THE WAR. BUT FIRST HE NEEDS THEIR APPROVAL.

ARE YOU **READY** TO BOW DOWN BEFORE ANTONY'S MISTRESS? WILL YOU STAND AND WATCH WHILE OUR EGYPTIAN ENEMIES **STEAL** OUR LANDS?

HE GOES TO THE TEMPLE OF THE WAR GODDESS, BELLONA.

TO DIP A LANCE IN FRESH BLOOD.

HE THEN PROCEEDS TO THE CENTRE OF ROME...

KILL THEM!

WAR!

NEVER!

NO!

WAR!

HE HAS WON THE CROWD.

BY MARCH 31 BC, ANTONY HAS SET UP A SERIES OF SEA BASES STRETCHING FROM CORFU ALL THE WAY TO THE NORTH AFRICAN COAST. IT IS NOW THAT **AGRIPPA** STRIKES.

WITHOUT WARNING, HIS NAVY APPEARS FROM ACROSS THE IONIAN SEA. FIRST HE TAKES THE FORT OF **METHONE**. FROM HERE, HE ATTACKS ANTONY'S OTHER NEARBY BASES AND BEGINS TO THREATEN THE SHIPS ON ANTONY'S **SUPPLY LINE**.

AT THEIR BASE IN PATRAE, GREECE, ANTONY AND CLEOPATRA BEGIN TO RUN SHORT OF **EVERYTHING**.

URRRGH!

WHATEVER'S THE MATTER, QUINTUS?

THIS WINE'S **SOUR**! IN **ROME** THEY STILL SERVE THE FINEST WINES!

NOW THEY ARE RUNNING SHORT OF **TIME**. OCTAVIAN LANDS HIS ARMY ON THE MAINLAND, NORTH OF CORFU. MARCHING QUICKLY, HE SOON HAS ANTONY'S BASE AT ACTIUM IN HIS SIGHTS.

ANTONY'S PLANS ARE FALLING APART. NOW HE BRINGS HIS NAVY THROUGH THE OPENING OF THE AMBRACIAN GULF TO SET UP HEADQUARTERS WITH CLEOPATRA ON THE SOUTHERN SIDE.

OCTAVIAN IS JOINED BY AGRIPPA, WHO ARRANGES THEIR SHIPS ACROSS THE ENTRANCE OF THE GULF. THIS TRAPS ANTONY'S NAVY FOR MORE THAN 16 WEEKS.

IN AUGUST, ANTONY CALLS A COUNCIL OF WAR...

WE **HAVE** TO BREAK OUT. SHOULD IT BE BY LAND OR SEA?

GENERAL CANIDIUS SPEAKS...

BY LAND! LEAVE THE SHIPS AND THE QUEEN **BEHIND**!

NO!

EGYPT HAS MUCH TOO HIGH A STAKE IN THIS WAR FOR YOU TO LEAVE ME BEHIND!

BY SEA IT IS THEN.

AFTER THE MEETING...

AT LEAST WE SHALL HAVE THE MAESTRO WIND WITH US...*

*AN OFF-SHORE BREEZE.

A FEW DAYS LATER, OCTAVIAN LEARNS OF THE PLAN FROM **QUINTUS DELLIUS**...

HE MEANS TO ESCAPE AND HAS ORDERED ALL SHIPS RIGGED WITH FULL SAILS.

TELL ME SOMETHING, QUINTUS. ANTONY'S YOUR FRIEND. **WHY** HAVE YOU BETRAYED HIM?

I INTEND TO BE ON THE WINNING SIDE.

2ND SEPTEMBER, 31 BC...

AS ANTONY'S SHIPS FILE OUT OF THE MOUTH OF THE GULF OF AMBRACIA, AGRIPPA ORDERS HIS NAVY TO FAN OUT INTO A WIDE CRESCENT TO FORM A BARRICADE. ANTONY'S FORCE SPREADS OUT TO FACE THEM, WHILE CLEOPATRA BRINGS UP THE REAR.

OCTAVIAN COMMANDS HIS FLAGSHIP...

THEN THEY MEET AND THE CENTRE LINE **PARTS.**

AT THE **REAR**, CLEOPATRA SEES HER CHANCE.

ROW BACKWARDS! DRAW THEM OUT!

MAKE FOR THAT GAP! FULL SPEED AHEAD!

THE QUEEN'S TREASURE SHIP, THE ANTONIAS, PASSES THROUGH...

...AND INTO THE OPEN SEA.

ON 1ST AUGUST, OCTAVIAN MARCHES INTO ALEXANDRIA, WITHOUT A FIGHT. ANTONY'S ARMIES HAVE LEFT HIM.

TODAY CAESAR HAS RESCUED THE STATE FROM ITS GRAVEST DANGER!

IN TIME, THE VICTORIOUS OCTAVIAN, OR CAESAR, WILL BECOME *AUGUSTUS,* THE FIRST EMPEROR OF ROME.

CLEOPATRA FLEES TO HER UNFINISHED MAUSOLEUM.

TELL ANTONY I AM DEAD!

ANTONY IS AT THE PALACE WITH HIS SERVANTS, WHEN HE HEARS.

EROS, HERE IS MY SWORD. **END ME!**

I REFUSE!

VERY WELL!

URRRGH!

THEN...

ANTONY! THE QUEEN IS ALIVE!

TAKE...ME ...TO HER.

ANTONY IS CARRIED INTO THE MAUSOLEUM.

I HAVE HAD THE GREATEST FAME AND POWER OF ANY MAN IN THE WORLD. I DIE WITHOUT DISHONOUR. DO NOT GRIEVE FOR ME, MY...**VENUS.**

GLOSSARY

abdication When a king or queen gives up their right to the throne.

ancestors Distant relatives of a person, farther back than grandparents.

astrologer A person who tries to tell the future by studying the movements of the stars and planets.

barricade A barrier put up to defend a place from attack.

catapult A machine used to launch missiles into the air.

cavalry The part of an army made up of troops on horseback.

chamberlain An officer who manages the household of a king or queen.

civil war A war between two armies from the same country.

cohort A unit of the Roman army, made up of about 1,000 men.

consul The most senior official in the Roman government who managed the army and Senate matters.

debt Something, usually money, that is owed to someone else.

dictator An official in the Roman government, during the Roman republic. He was appointed in times of crisis.

Dionysus A Greek god, who became linked to the Roman god, Bacchus, and the Egyptian god, Osiris.

Donations Gifts of lands and titles given to Cleopatra and her children by Mark Antony.

dynasty A line of leaders from the same family group.

exile Being officially banished or sent away from one's home as a form of punishment.

flagship The ship belonging to a fleet's commander.

flotilla A small fleet of ships or boats.

garrison The troops who guard a base or fort.

incense A material that is burned to make a strong, pleasant smell.

legacies Gifts of money, land, or property given when someone dies.

legion A unit of the Roman army, made up of about 5,000 men.

mausoleum A large tomb.

mercenaries Troops hired to fight in a foreign army.

mutiny When soldiers rebel or refuse to obey their commanders.

pharaohs Rulers of Ancient Egypt.

province A country or region that was brought under the control of the Roman government.

regent An official who rules on behalf of a king or queen.

revenge To get even with someone who has hurt you by doing something unpleasant to them.

siege When an army surrounds a city and does not let supplies of food or water in until the city surrenders.

toga A loose wrap worn as an outer garment by Romans.

Venus The Roman goddess of love and beauty.

FOR MORE INFORMATION

ORGANISATIONS

The British Museum
Great Russell Street
London
WC1B 3DG
www.thebritishmuseum.ac.uk

Ashmolean Museum of Art and Archaeology
Beaumont Street
Oxford
OX1 2PH
www.ashmol.ox.ac.uk

FOR FURTHER READING
If you liked this book, you might also want to try:

How to be an Ancient Egyptian Princess
by Jacquline Morley, Book House 2005

How to be a Roman Soldier
by Fiona Macdonald, Book House 2005

Battle Zones: Warfare in the Ancient World
by Mark Bergin, Book House 2003

Avoid becoming an Egyptian Pyramid Builder!
by Jacqueline Morley, Book House 2003

INDEX

Websites

Due to the changing nature of Internet links, the Salariya Book Company, has developed an online list of websites related to the subject of this book. This site is updated regularly. Please use this link to access the list:

http://www.book-house.co.uk/gnf/cleo